INDIAN NATIONS

The Story of the Sioux

They called themselves Dakota, which meant "friends," but the Chippewa, with whom they were often at war, called them Sioux, which meant "enemies." Sioux is the name that stayed with the seven large bands of Indians who migrated to the prairie when it was black with buffalo. This is their story, how they came on foot to the plains, how they met the white man and his horse, became expert horsemen, and lived well and free until there were too many white men and not enough buffalo.

The Story of the SIOUX

by the Editors of
COUNTRY BEAUTIFUL
Text by Marion E. Gridley

Illustrations by Robert Glaubke

G. P. Putnam's Sons   *New York*

in association with Country Beautiful Corporation,
Waukesha, Wisconsin

Contents

The Story of the SIOUX

is the latest volume in a series of authentic books about INDIAN NATIONS that have made significant contributions to our heritage and also are representative of particular cultures.

The Editors of *Country Beautiful* recommend the new titles, all written by Marion E. Gridley and published by G. P. Putnam's Sons in association with the Country Beautiful Corporation.

INDIAN NATIONS:

The Story of the IROQUOIS

The Story of the NAVAJO

The Story of the SIOUX

The Story of the HAIDA

The Story of the SEMINOLE

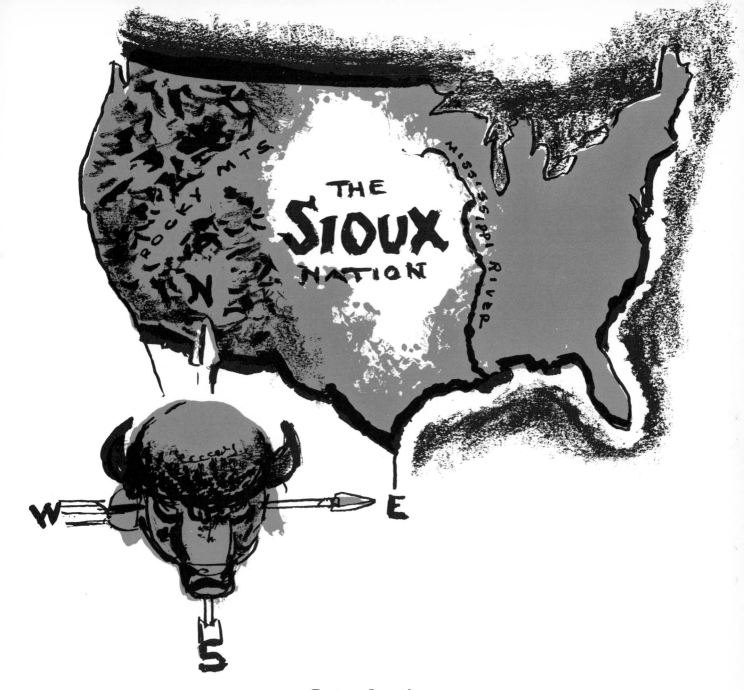

Introduction

It is believed that the first home of the American Indians was in northern Asia. In a search of food and better living conditions, these early people followed the game animals and are said to have crossed over the narrow strait between Siberia and Alaska. It was thousands of years after this crossing was made that there was movement still farther into the continent.

All alone in the New World, the first people continued to travel and to separate into groups of families. They had fire; they fished and hunted; they made spears and clubs for weapons. When the separations took place, the people began to change. They went into different parts of the country, and they adapted their way of life according to the conditions that were found.

The groups began to speak differently, dress differently, and live differently from one another. They had different names for themselves, and mostly these names meant "the chosen people." In some things the people were alike, for they kept a sameness that went back to ancient ways, but they were not alike in other habits that were influenced by their new surroundings.

This book is about one large tribe, the Sioux. Living in the eastern woodlands until pushed out by other Indians, the Sioux came to the Great Plains, or prairie country, between the Rocky Mountains and the Mississippi River. At first the Sioux were afraid of the flat land, open to the sky and to the winds and seemingly without end. After a time, they ventured upon it and found good hunting grounds. They roamed over the vast area and developed a hunting way of life, entirely suited to the land which was now theirs.

1.

The Sioux Indians

The Sioux Indians call themselves Dakota, which means "friends" or "allies." The name "Sioux" comes from a long Chippewa word which means "they are our enemies." The two tribes were always at war.

The Sioux are made up of seven large bands, independent and self-ruling but thinking of themselves as one people. They roamed over a large part of what is now the two Dakota states, Nebraska, and western Montana.

When the Sioux first moved onto the prairie, they found the bison, or buffalo. One buffalo provided meat for a family for a long time. As far as the eye could see, the land was black with buffalo. Sometimes one herd grazed over an area ten miles long and eight miles wide and numbered as many as 2,000,000 or more of the huge, shaggy animals.

It was not easy to kill the buffalo with just flint-headed spears for weapons. Hunters, disguised in wolfskins, managed to creep close enough to the animals to spear a few. Sometimes they drove some animals away from the herd and over a cliff or into a corral. The injured could then be destroyed.

So that they could stay close to the buffalo herds and follow them when the animals moved to find fresh grass

and water, the Indians lived in small brush or skin shel-
ters. They had few household goods because it was not
possible to carry much. Dogs were used as pack animals.
Family belongings were placed on a rack fastened to
two poles which were lashed to a dog and pulled along
the ground. The dogs could carry heavy loads in this
way, but they could walk only five or six miles in a day.
The people could not go very fast or very far, and the
buffalo could leave them a long way behind. The Indians
knew nothing of wheels or wagons and never invented
them.

When the Spaniards came to America, they brought
horses with them. Some of these horses ran away and
were captured by Indians. Many tribes then lived on
the Plains, and once they had horses, there developed
a Plains Indian way of living found nowhere else.

With horses, the Sioux became true wanderers, going
where they wished and following the buffalo wherever

it led. A horse could be trained to run close beside a buffalo so that a hunter could make his kill. A horse could carry four times as much as a dog could and twice as far. Because the people could keep pace with the buffalo, there was always food.

The Sioux raised no crops, made no pottery or baskets. They were constantly on the move and seldom stayed long in one place. Their once-small tents became large and comfortable but were still movable dwellings. Everything worn or used was made of skin. The men became expert horsemen. They rode as though horse and rider were one.

The Sioux called the horses, which changed their entire manner of life, spirit dogs or elk dogs. The horses were the wealth of the tribe, but the life of the people centered on the buffalo. Horse and buffalo together were loved by the Sioux as nothing else could be loved or honored.

2.

The Wonderful Buffalo

Without the buffalo, the Sioux people could not have lived. All that they had or needed came from the animal. The Sioux and the buffalo were never separated. The animal was thought to be a special gift from the Great Spirit, sent to serve and help the Indians.

The buffalo understood this, the Sioux believed, and were willing to be sacrificed for the good of the Sioux. The Indians could not foresee that someday the buffalo would be destroyed.

First of all, the buffalo was food. Every part of the buffalo was eaten. For winter use, the meat was sliced thin, dried in the sun, and stored. It was made into pemmican by pounding and mixing the dried meat with dried, crushed berries, melted fat and marrow.

Buffalo hides were used to make the Indian tepees, or tents, and the droppings of the animals were the fuel for fire, since there were few trees on the plains. Hides with the hair left on made warm winter robes and bed coverings.

The untanned hide could be hardened until it was like a stiff board. This had many uses. It was fashioned into boxes and cases for storing articles, clothing and food.

It was made into cooking kettles and into round tublike boats. The Sioux did not travel along rivers as the Eastern Indians did. They crossed them, and so large boats were not necessary.

Rawhide was good for sturdy moccasin soles, for shields and quivers, for arrows, and for backing bows to make them stronger. Rawhide was used to cover saddles and for the heads of drums. Thongs for lacing and tying, robes, and the webbing of snowshoes all came from this material.

The horns of the buffalo made fine drinking cups and spoons. They were cut into small pieces and strung into a jingling necklace. The Sioux believed that the buffalo knew how to cure broken bones and injuries. The buffalo doctors were supposed to learn this art from the animal. They wore buffalo horn headdresses and stamped their feet and roared like buffalo when they danced their healing dances.

For broken bones, the buffalo doctors were expert at splinting with rawhide and in setting them properly so that they would knit straight and strong.

A good glue came from the hooves of the buffalo. Bow strings and thread for sewing came from the tendons, or sinews. Sleds for children were made from the ribs. Needles were made from sharpened bits of bone.

It is no wonder that the Sioux were so dependent on the huge creature. They danced in honor of the buffalo and prayed to it. They sang songs about the buffalo. There was nothing as wonderful as the wonderful buffalo.

3.

The Take-Along House

The Indian tepee was ideal for nomadic living. It was cool in summer and warm in winter. It was both a house and a means of transportation.

The tepee framework of tall poles was tied together at the top, and the lower ends were spread out to form a large circle. About twenty poles, 18 to 20 feet long, were used. They were straight, slim young trees that would not bend. The Indians had to travel to the mountains to get them.

It took at least twenty buffalo hides to make the covering of the tepee. The women tanned the hides to a gleaming whiteness. When a new cover was made, the women held a sewing bee. The skins were cut and shaped by older women, who were skilled in this work. When the cover was finished, the tepee owner gave a feast to thank the women for completing it.

The tepee cover was held fast to the ground by stakes around the edge. Inside, a ground stake held a rope fas-

tened to the top of the poles. This anchored the tepee against the strong prairie winds. The front of the cover was pinned together with long wooden pins, or skewers.

At the top of the tepee, two flaps like wings were held upright by poles. The flaps could be moved around as the wind changed to let out the smoke from the center fire. They were closed over each other in bad weather to keep out rain or snow.

The tepee door was an oval opening covered with an animal skin. In hot weather, the edges of the tepee were raised to let in air. In the winter, a skin lining around the inside gave extra warmth.

There was no furniture. Beds made of grass were placed around the sides and were used for both sitting and sleeping. Backrests of a stick framework made sitting more comfortable. Buffalo robe covers gave the beds firmness.

When the camp moved, the tepee poles were fastened into a V shape and placed on the back of a pony with ends dragging on the ground, just as had been done when dogs were the carriers. The pony drag was called a travois. The tepee cover was folded and placed on the travois rack with other articles, and the people were ready to go.

Several women working together could take the tepee down or set it up within three minutes. The women owned their tepees and everything in them.

The men painted designs on the outsides of the tepee which told of their adventures as warriors, or symbolized their names, or described a dream or vision. The women decorated the inside.

A tepee camp was always in the form of a circle, just as the tepee was a circle. The circle had sacred meaning. It stood for protection, for the sun and the earth from which all life came were circles. It stood for the unity of the people, for the circle was an unbroken line holding good within and keeping evil out.

The tepees of the chiefs were in the inner part of the circle. At the outer rim were those of the soldier-braves who were the camp policemen. All tepees faced the east.

A large village of a thousand tepees or more was a beautiful sight. The skin covers gleamed in the sunshine, and the tepees were gracefully formed. At night, with fires burning inside, they looked like huge lanterns.

4.

Life in a Tepee Village

"Hey! Hey! Hey! Get ready! Get ready! The buffalo move!" The village crier shouted out the news. The buffalo watchers, who stayed near the herds, had signaled to watchers in the village, and there was no time to be lost.

At once, the camp was plunged into activity. The women and girls ran to pack up the family belongings and to take down the tepees. The young men and boys hurried to round up the horse herd and to bring up the horses which would be ridden. The women saddled their horses, but the men rode without saddles.

Travois were put in place, and babies, in their cradleboards, were hung from their mothers' saddles. A small child rode in the saddle with his mother, too, or on a travois with an older person who could no longer ride horseback.

Ahead of the people went the scouts, who would be on the lookout for enemies and who would choose the

21

new campsite. Following them were the village chiefs and the soldier-braves. Ranging on each side of the women and children, horses and camp dogs were heavily armed warriors ready to defend the people from any attack.

The last to leave the village was the fire bearer who made certain that every fire was out. He took with him a few coals in a buffalo horn which he would use to light new fires when the camp was again set up.

Life in the village began at dawn. First, the people bathed in the nearby stream. The daily bath was a ritual both summer and winter, but it could be done only downstream from where drinking water was taken.

On the day that a buffalo hunt would take place, the camp crier announced this and the rules of the hunt.

The hunt began only when the headman signaled for it to start. No one could start out on his own or disturb the herd in any way. The soldier-braves would severely punish any man who did so. His weapons were destroyed, his clothing was torn, his tepee pulled down, and he was in deep disgrace.

Each hunter marked his arrows so that he could identify his kill. Those who could not hunt for themselves never went hungry, for it was the duty of the strong to share with those who were not.

When the hunt was over, the women skinned the dead animals, cut up the meat, and carried it back to the camp on packhorses. For days after, they tanned hides, made new clothes, and prepared the meat for winter.

Aside from the hunt, the soldier-braves had other

23

duties. They saw to it that tepees were pitched right and were in proper position and that the campgrounds were clean. They did not permit quarreling among the people. They said where horses were to be pastured and who was to watch over the herd at night.

During the pleasant months, there were many feasts and ceremonies and other social activities. The men would go on horse-stealing raids or on war parties. There were games and sports of all kinds: wrestling, riding, swimming or shooting contests, games of ball and of dice, and guessing games.

Although the Sioux were meat eaters and never fished, they did have other food. There were roots, wild fruit and berries and other plants that were good for eating. Wild beans and wild potatoes were gathered and a wild turnip, which the Sioux called *Teepsinna*. This looked something like a peanut with a smooth shell. Birds' eggs and waterfowl were also eaten.

The Sioux were fond of corn, but they had to trade for this with those tribes who grew it.

Since the people had to make everything they had, men and women, old and young were constantly busy. Life was not all moving and raiding and hunting. No one could be idle or live idly, but there was always time for the people to enjoy and to help one another.

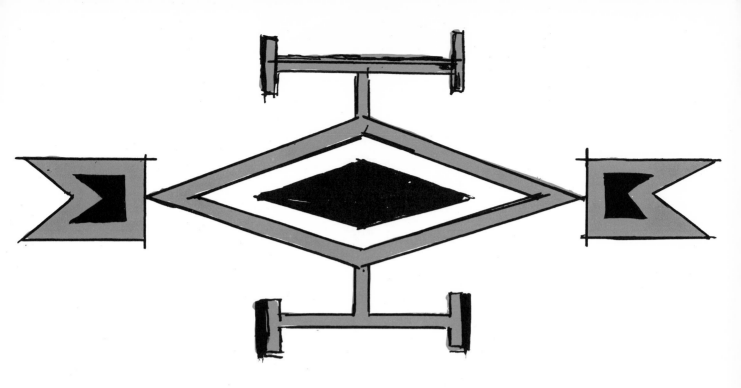

5.

How the Sioux Dressed

Because of their handsome appearance and picturesque clothes, their wonderful ability as horsemen, and their great fame as warriors, the Plains Indians came to typify all Indians of America.

Most of the time, the Sioux men wore only a breechclout and moccasins. Faces and body were painted with meaningful designs, both in daily life and for war.

For dress occasions or in cold weather, the men wore leggings with wide, fringed flaps. These protected their legs when riding horseback and were copied by the American cowboys. A shirt of two skins sewn together with an opening for the head was worn with these leggings. Later sleeves were added which were fringed at the sides and sometimes trimmed with long strips of weasel skin

25

or with bits of dyed horsehair. The bottom edges of the shirt were also fringed, and a breastplate of polished deer bones and a breechclout completed the costume. A great warrior might wear a necklace of bear claws.

26

Women wore moccasins, short leggings, and throughout the year a dress made of two skins forming a skirt with a third skin going over the head in a loose, capelike yoke. The side seams and bottom of the skirt were fringed, and a wide belt was worn about the waist. Carefully spaced elk teeth were sewn to the dress for decoration.

Even when the women got blue and red trader cloth from the white settlers, they still preferred their beautiful skin clothes for festive times. The cloth dresses, also decorated with elk teeth, were for everyday use.

Buffalo skin was too heavy for clothing, so deer and elk skins were used. The men painted symbols of their outstanding deeds on the inside of their buffalo hide winter robes just as the tepee was painted. Women painted their robes with a sunburst design.

Both men and women wore their hair in two braids or loose and flowing. The young men wore a deer tail roach on their heads, but the women wore nothing in their hair. Sometimes they wrapped their braids in fur, or in a piece of beaded cloth, or tied them at the ear with large ornaments.

In early contact with the white men, the Eastern Indians obtained small glass beads with which they decorated their clothing. When beads finally reached the Plains country, the women became the finest bead workers in the world.

Beadwork was an ideal craft for the Sioux people. The beads were easily carried and no other equipment, such as a loom, was needed. Sioux beadwork differed from woodland beadwork in the method of sewing and in the designs. Where the Eastern Indians used floral and scroll designs, the Sioux women used squares, triangles, oblongs, and combinations of these. Such designs are called geometric.

All Indian beadwork is a substitution of beads for dyed porcupine quills or animal hair, but the work was definitely Indian in creation, even though beads could be obtained only from the white man.

When the women became skilled in using the tiny beads, everything was beaded. The men had bands of beadwork over the shoulders and down the sleeves of their shirts and down the sides of their leggings. Moccasins and the yolks of women's dresses were solidly beaded. A baby's cradleboard was covered with beading. Horses were adorned with beadwork. Anything that could be beaded was beaded. The Sioux were fond of using light-blue or white beads for backgrounds and strong colors for their designs.

6.
Warriors and Eagle Feathers

The majestic eagle feather headdress worn by the Sioux warrior was the most spectacular part of his costume. It was this headdress, so much admired by Indians and whites alike, that preserved the image of the Plains Indian and established this image for all America. Today every Indian who can wears a feather headdress because it is expected of him and because it has become Indian fashion.

In the old days among the Sioux, not even a chief

could wear a feather headdress unless he had earned
the right to do so. The headdress was like the Congres-
sional Medal of Honor. It was the symbol of the highest
bravery and heroism, the mark of a man above men.

To understand why the eagle feather was so highly
thought of, the Indian feeling for the eagle must be understood. The eagle was a fierce fighting bird, so powerful
that it could kill a person if angered. It was a bird of
mystery, for no other bird could fly so high or so far

or build its nest in the mountain peaks. It was an extremely dangerous task to trap an eagle, and only certain men of the tribe were allowed to do this.

Among the Sioux, going to war was the most important of all the man's activities. It was a career in which he won personal fame, for no Sioux ever went to war without the hope of achieving honors. War was a glorified game, and no Sioux ever entered into it just for the sole purpose of killing.

The Sioux did not fight to capture prisoners and rarely took them. They did not fight to get slaves, for they had no need of them. Unless it was a matter of a battle for revenge or with traditional enemies, most Sioux war parties were small and intent only on horse raiding.

To touch an enemy in battle with the hand or with a special stick or whip was considered the bravest of all acts of warfare. This was called "counting coup." To kill someone took far less courage, and to scalp a dead enemy involved no risk at all. The warrior who counted coup was entitled to one eagle feather tipped with eagle down or horsehair. If he also killed the man whom he touched, a red spot was placed on the feather.

A notched eagle feather meant that the warrior had cut the throat of an enemy. The warrior who was wounded in battle was awarded a feather split down the middle.

Every deed of daring had a definitive feather value and style of feather. After counting ten coups, a warrior could wear the feather headdress if the council of warriors, who had also earned this right, agreed that he might do so. Counting coup was so great an accomplishment that no warrior would lie about having done so. He could be challenged in the council meeting, and if

proved untruthful, he would be severely punished. All previously won honors of any kind would be taken from him and he would be shunned by his people.

After a battle, no man was modest. He was expected to describe what he had done before the whole tribe and even to act it out, but he was not allowed to be continuously boastful.

The Sioux war party generally engaged in a surprise attack at dawn. The warriors always prepared themselves with special ceremonies before leaving. They danced war dances and sang war songs. Each man sang the song that he owned and which no one else could sing, or the songs of the military society to which he belonged. He might sing: "If there is anything hard or dangerous, that is for me to do." Or he might sing: "It is good to die young in battle. I am ready to die."

In fighting, it was every man for himself. If the "signs" were bad, a warrior could refuse to go with a war party or a war party might be called off. The warrior who would not fight because of a warning dream or vision was never looked down upon or considered a coward.

No Sioux warrior would go into battle without his shield, which was a sacred object. Like the sun, the shield was round and was painted with dream or vision designs. The shield was thought to have great spiritual power.

The Sioux firmly believed in the power of their shields, and they carried them into battle against the white soldiers, certain that they would be protected. The shield could protect the warrior from arrows, but against bullets they were useless. Many lives were lost in Indian-white battles because the Sioux relied so strongly on their shields.

7.

A Language of Signals

The Sioux people developed a system of signals, for the wide and open country in which they lived made it possible to signal from great distances. The movements of a horse and rider, the tossing of a robe or a blanket, puffs of smoke from a fire were ways by which scouts could send information and messages. A horse ridden in a circle meant: "Keep watching. A message is coming." When an answering signal came, the message was sent.

Later in their history, the Sioux used small mirrors, which they got from white traders, for signaling. A warrior was never without his mirror. It became a part of his costume, and the men often admired themselves in their mirrors when dancing the war dance.

Indian tribes do not speak the same language, and on the Plains more than twenty languages were spoken. To a people used to communicating with signals, it was natural to invent a signal "speech." This sign language was an invention of the Plains groups and was not known by other Indians.

With hand talk, a whole new means of understanding was created, making it possible for strangers to meet and become friends because they could speak together. Long conversations could be held in great detail without one spoken word. The motions formed pictures which were very clear and unmistakable, and the movements were graceful. Indian hand talk is said to be the best of any gesture language.

When strangers met, it was customary to raise the open hand in greeting. This was a sign of peace, for the hand held no weapon. The waving of the hand back and forth meant that talk was to begin. It was also used to ask a question.

The sign language was also valuable in war, for warriors could relay messages without having to speak. At night, there was a system of handclasps and grips, body tappings and finger tracings through which warriors could maintain contact.

8.

Growing Up

Sioux children were seldom punished but were taught by example. The children were thought of as the future of the tribe, and it was impressed upon them in every way that they must serve their people from whom they could never be separated. The most dreadful punishment that could be inflicted upon an adult who went against tribal law was banishment from the group. No person cared to risk this.

Indian babies were placed in a cradleboard at birth and remained in it until they were at least two. They were taken out to be bathed and to exercise, but while

they were in the cradle, they were safe, yet they were a part of everything that went on.

As soon as a Sioux child began to talk, he was also taught to dance, and he learned games that were imitations of an adult's daily life. Games were fun, but they all taught something. Dancing was a method of keeping physically fit, and all religious ceremonies were dances.

Boys had to grow up hardy and strong, so they were very early taught lessons of bravery. As soon as a boy could sit on a horse, he was taught how to ride and

38

how to fall off without injury. Boys played at mock battles, learning how to scout and how to track by footprints. Every tribe had its own moccasin shape, and a boy had to know how to recognize it. Animals were tracked by their footprints, too, and these had to be identified as the animal they belonged to.

At six, a boy got his first bow and a girl got her first doll. When he was twelve, a boy was given a real bow, for by then he had become a good shot. He now watched the family horse herds and had his own horse which he cared for. He could go with the men on hunting parties, and he followed his father on the buffalo hunt, watching what went on from the sidelines and bringing down a straggling calf on his own.

If at any time a boy was hurt, he was not permitted to cry out or to admit he was in pain. It was only the weakling who gave in to suffering.

When he shot his first buffalo, a boy's family gave a feast in his honor. He had to give away the best parts of the meat to those invited to the feast, and presents and horses were also given away. In this way the boy was taught to share. At this time he also had to sacrifice that which he loved the most or which meant the most to him. If this was a beloved pet or a favorite horse, it would be ceremonially killed. This sacrifice was the boy's first offering to the Great Spirit. It had to be done without sorrow and with great reverence as an expression of love for the one to whom the Indian people looked for all good.

Very soon after this took place, a boy was taken on his first raid. He cooked for the men, brought water, ran errands, and carried the things which might be needed. Yet all the time, he was learning what a warrior did and the skills of the braves.

When the boy became a youth, he was sent away from the village to fast and to plead for a vision. It was not until a vision had come that he was fully accepted as grown or taken into the young men's societies. Whatever appeared to him in his vision was ever after his spirit helper. He would be given a name based on this vision to replace the birth name, which indicated his place in the family as first-, second-, third-, or last-born son. He could receive other names during his lifetime—nick-

names or deed names—but the spirit name was his true name.

Sioux girls learned to do everything around the home. They did not belong to societies, and they remained close to their mothers until a marriage was arranged for them.

9.

Storytelling

Part of a child's teaching came through storytelling. At night the family gathered in the tepee while an older person repeated tales of the long ago. They were about the Sioux heroes and their great deeds or how things had come to be. Many of the stories were about animals, so the children learned how they looked and their habits. Hunters had to know all about animals. The hunter had great respect for the animals, and they did not kill them unless it was necessary to do so for food. The animals were very smart and could outwit hunters who were not familiar with how the animals behaved.

Stories that were told especially for the children were those about Iktomi, the spider. Iktomi did many foolish things. He was a trickster and used his wits to cheat others. He was dirty and lazy—not at all as an Indian was and should be. The stories taught the children that they must not be like Iktomi who never gained from his badness. There were many stories about Iktomi, and some were quite long.

One of the Iktomi stories had two parts. In the first part, Iktomi was very hungry, for he had been a long time without food. He started out to see what he could find that would make a good dinner.

Iktomi came to a river and there were some ducks swimming and diving in the water. "Fine!" Iktomi thought. "Just what I wanted—roast duck."

Quickly Iktomi ran back to his lodge, where he got a deerskin and filled it with grass. He tied the skin into a bundle, which he carried on his shoulder. When he got back to where the ducks were, he walked right by them as if he did not see them.

The ducks called to him. "Where are you going, Iktomi? What do you have in your bundle?"

"Nothing that would interest you, little brothers," Iktomi replied.

The ducks crowded around Iktomi and begged to see. Iktomi said he had only some old songs, and he promised to sing them for the ducks if they would build a lodge and dance for him while he sang.

This was soon done. When all the ducks were inside, Iktomi covered the door with the deerskin so that it was dark. Then he said: "Now I will sing, and you will dance, but you must keep your eyes tightly closed or you will have red eyes forever."

As the ducks danced around in a circle, Iktomi would grab a fat one and wring its neck. Soon he had a pile of fat ducks. Then one duck opened its eyes and saw what was happening.

"Fly, brothers! Fly! Iktomi is killing us!" the duck screeched.

The ducks knocked Iktomi down and scratched him with their feet and beat at him with their wings in their haste to get away. As they flew away, they looked at each other and said: "Brothers, your eyes are red." Some ducks do have red eyes, and the Indians say that is how they got them.

In the second part of the story, Iktomi has roasted the ducks and is about to eat them, when along comes a pack of wolves. They chased Iktomi up into a tree and ate the ducks while Iktomi cried and wailed and begged them not to. Now and again, they threw Iktomi a bone, smacking their lips over the good food.

When they left, they thanked Iktomi for inviting them to a duck feast.

Poor Iktomi! He had been badly beaten up by the ducks, he had lost his dinner to the wolves, and once again he was hungry.

10.
The Great Sun Dance

During the year, the Sioux people held many feasts and ceremonies. There were some which were purely social and which provided the people with entertainment. There were others which were highly religious.

The buffalo ceremony was both to honor the buffalo and to bring the buffalo back after their winter migration. The horse dance honored the horse and was also a prayer for rain. In this dance, riders painted themselves the color of the horses they rode. There were four black horses, four white, four sorrel, or roan, and four buckskin, or golden tan.

Four young women dressed in red-dyed skin dresses with wreaths of sage on their heads led the horse dancers

onto the field. The women's faces were painted scarlet. Six drummers stood around a large drum, chanting and pounding out the rhythm for the dance.

The bear dance was a healing ceremony and a religious rite. It was also done when an individual wished to announce himself as a medicine man, or doctor, who had received his medical powers from the bear.

The maidens' feast was given during the summer by the young maidens as a sort of "coming out" party.

There were many giveaways in which the wealthier families gave away the best of what they had, and often everything they had. Valuable gifts, horses, and other possessions were given to those in need, never to relatives or to those who had plenty. At every public event there always had to be a distribution of fine presents.

The biggest and most important of all giveaways was the sun dance held each summer. This was a great religious ceremony when all the Sioux bands gathered to take part for success in war and hunting or for good health.

Long before the time, the leaders of the dance had chosen the place where it would be held. When all the Sioux came together, a very large campsite would be required with lots of grass for horses and plenty of water close by.

About a month ahead of the date for the dance, messengers were sent to Sioux villages wherever they were. A space was cleared in the center of where the tepees would be set up, and here the round sun dance lodge was built. Only the men could take part in the dance, and only those who had made earlier vows to do so.

Everything in connection with the dance was done in fours. It took four days and nights to build the lodge,

48

and there were four days of getting ready for the cere-mony. Four was a sacred number, the Indians said, because the Great Spirit had created everything in fours. There are four directions, four seasons, four elements, and four parts to everything that grows. There are four kinds of creatures on the earth and four periods in human life among other symbolic reasons.

Because they were asking blessings, the dancers also had to sacrifice and to prove themselves men. During one part of the ceremony, they were fastened to the sun dance pole by long ropes skewered through their chest muscles. Throughout the ceremony, the dancers blew on eagle bone whistles and, in spite of their pain, danced until the skewers tore through the skin and they were free. They took no food or water in the entire time. If a dancer went through the whole four days, he knew that his prayers would be answered.

The sun dance time was a celebration. Marriages took place; families held giveaways; other tribes came to visit and were royally entertained. There was only goodwill and happiness. No war parties or raiders went out, and no enemy would attack a sun dance camp.

When the sun dance ended, the sun dance chief blessed the people and they departed. They had to leave because the horses had eaten all the grass at hand.

11.
Gone the Buffalo—Gone Freedom

Into the Plains country came many white men. They built forts on Indian land; they hunted for gold and furs; they made a railroad. Worst of all, they killed off the buffalo. This, to the Indians, was tragedy.

Hemmed in closer and closer by the invading whites, the Indians fought to defend themselves and their homes. Brave as they were and as fine fighters, the Sioux could not stand up against many soldiers armed with guns or against the starvation that faced them when the buffalo vanished.

There was constant fighting until General George Custer marched his troops to the Little Bighorn River in Montana. Custer and the soldiers were wiped out by the Sioux in a great Indian victory.

This was also the last stand of the Indians, for even though they won, they lost. The shock of Custer's defeat brought out government troops in full force, and Indians were harried from one end of the Plains to the other. Some of the Sioux escaped into Canada.

One by one, the tribes were broken, for there was not enough food with the buffalo gone and there was not enough room to wander. One by one, the tribes agreed to lay down their weapons and to live on small areas of land called reservations. The Sioux were the last to surrender and to accept reservation life.

To keep them from starving, the government issued food rations while the brokenhearted people watched the cattle ranchers take over their boundless plains. In despair, the Sioux looked for a new leader and found

51

him in Wovoka, a Paiute, who brought a new religion. The Indians were told that they must live in peace, have no more to do with war, and that they would be led to a new world. There they would find their own people and there would be no whites to torment them.

Faithfully, the Sioux danced the new ghost dance as they waited for all this to come about.

Like the sun dance, the ghost dance was a test of physical endurance. Both men and women danced and took no food or water. They hoped to fall in a trance and to see a vision of loved ones who were dead, or the buffalo, or other reminders of the happy olden days of the mighty Sioux, now a pitiful, hungry few.

The whites did not understand the meaning of the ghost dance and thought that the Indians secretly plotted war while they danced. Soldiers were sent to surround the ghost dance camp and to order the Indians to give up any arms they might have.

While the soldiers looked for hidden guns by destroying the camp, fighting broke out and more than two hundred Indians were mowed down by Army guns. Back to their reservations the remaining Sioux went, and from then on they lived in no other way.

For the Sioux and other Plains tribes, adjustment to the new way of life was extremely hard—much harder than it had been for other Indians. They tried to learn how to farm, but they were not a farming people and never had been. The hunter and warrior found no joy in following a plow. Planting was not for men. The yearning for the freedom that had been theirs was almost unbearable. Freedom and the buffalo were gone forever.

Somehow the Sioux survived through a period of great trouble and suffering. The ghost dance grounds at

Wounded Knee Creek was the burial place of all that had been Indian greatness, but the spirit of the people remained strong, and they helped themselves, as they had always done, make the best of what was left to them.

Sitting
Bull

12.

Some Famous Sioux

There were many great leaders among the Sioux, and they made a deep impression on the records of history. Some of the famous ones were Young Man Afraid of His Horses, Red Cloud, Rain-in-the-Face, Crazy Horse and Gall.

Sitting Bull is probably the best known of all because he united the Sioux to resist and because of the part he played in the Custer affair and afterward. Sitting Bull was not a chief but a medicine man. It was he who led his people north into Canada in flight from the pursuing soldiers, and it was he who finally brought them home again to accept reservation life.

For a time, Sitting Bull traveled with Buffalo Bill's Wild West Show. Crowds of people flocked to see him, and most admired the proud Sioux. It was sad to see him in the role of a show Indian.

When Sitting Bull returned to the reservation, he settled down and did not take part in any of the ghost dance activity. Nevertheless, he was blamed for it. In an attempt to arrest him, he was killed. This, more than anything else, helped break Indian strength and end all fighting.

Chief Gall and Crazy Horse were the ones who led the Sioux charge against Custer and brought temporary victory out of what seemed certain destruction for the Indians. Both have been cited for their military genius. Crazy Horse won fame as a warrior when he was very young and fought under Red Cloud.

Crazy Horse was one of the last of the Sioux to lay

Red Cloud

down his weapons. He wanted to fight to the death, but he gave up for the sake of the suffering women and children. Like Sitting Bull, he was shot in what was mistakenly thought to be an escape attempt. As he lay dying, Crazy Horse said: "Tell the people I have done the best I could."

A memorial statue to Crazy Horse is in construction on Thunderhead Mountain in the Black Hills of South Dakota. It will be one of the world's largest statues. The sculptor shows Crazy Horse mounted on horseback and pointing to the land below as if he were repeating what he said when he surrendered: "My lands are where my dead lie buried."

One of the most famous Sioux in modern times, Dr. Charles A. Eastman, or Ohiyesa, the winner, was sixteen

Rain-in-the-Face

years old before he ever saw a white man. He was reared entirely in the old buffalo hunting ways, but he walked 150 miles to enter a mission school when he was seen that a new trail would have to be followed. He was sent from there to Beloit and Knox colleges and graduated from Dartmouth and from Boston University School of Medicine. He was appointed physician to the Sioux on the Pine Ridge Reservation and was there during the ghost dance massacre.

Dr. Eastman became the author of nine books, two of which were the story of his life. He lectured throughout the country and abroad and received many honors. In 1933 he was awarded the first of the annual Indian Achievement medals presented by the Indian Council Fire, a national Indian-interest organization.

A famous Sioux of today is Oscar Howe, an internationally recognized artist of great talent. Congressman Ben Reifel is the only Indian in the United States House of Representatives. There are many other Sioux who have won honors and who hold important positions in various professions.

Crazy Horse

13.

The Sioux Today

The Sioux now live on eight reservations in South Dakota, one in North Dakota and one straddling the North-South Dakota boundary, one in Montana, one in Nebraska, and in a few small communities in Minnesota.

The reservations come under the Bureau of Indian Affairs, which administers tribal property and which provides a number of special services, among them education. The bureau maintains both day and boarding schools, but nearly half the Indian children now attend public school. There are also mission schools on the reservations.

The medical care of the reservation Indians is the responsibility of the U.S. Public Health Service, which provides several hospitals and a program of health service and education.

On the reservations, the Indians can hunt or fish at any time if the rights granted in treaties made with the government are still in effect. There is little opportunity for employment, for the lands are bleak and in isolated areas and they are not large enough to sustain more than half the people living there.

When the reservations were established, it was thought that the Indians were a dying people. No plan was made for population growth beyond what then existed. With so little land, it is difficult to start cattle or farming enterprises of any economic value to the people as a whole. Much of the Indian land has been divided among family heirs, and no one gains any benefit from his small portion.

Some of the Sioux have become successful farmers and stock raisers, but on the whole the people have little beyond the bare necessities of life. They do not receive any financial support from the government but are eligible for federal, state, and local relief or welfare programs.

Housing programs have now been started on some of the reservations, and a few industries have been established in an attempt to bring revenue to the tribe and income to the people.

Among the Sioux, much of the "old Indian" pridefully remains. Most people have both an Indian and an English name. Many of the older women continue to wear Indian-style clothing with a colorful shawl in summer and a blanket in winter. The men dress like Western-style cowboys. A good many of the people still speak their own language, though it is being lost among the younger generation. Outside some of the homes, a tepee stands, for the older members of the family like to live in these the year round.

The close family ties which were so important in the buffalo days are still important. For this reason, Indians are reluctant to leave for employment in the cities, although many have. Most have adapted to city life and are doing well, though some, unused to the city, find it overwhelming and are often discriminated against.

The annual sun dance, at one time banned by the government, has been revived and is generally held each August. Around the sun dance camp, tents are set up instead of tepees, and there are more cars and trailers than horses.

Tourists are welcome to visit the reservations and to attend any ceremonies. They find the Sioux are still a proud people. Most know the history of their tribe, but they have gone proudly forth to volunteer as soldiers, sailors, airmen, and nurses in each of the wars since World War I. Even though they have little, they are generous in sharing what they have, for this is their way from ancient times.

Index

The Author

MARION E. GRIDLEY has always been interested in Indian culture and is an adopted member of two tribes—the Omaha and the Winnebago. She and her parents founded the Indian Council Fire, a national Indian-interest organization of Indian and white membership, and Miss Gridley has served as executive secretary of the organization since its inception. Miss Gridley is the editor and publisher of *The Amerindian*, a bimonthly information bulletin on Indians. She is the author of *The Story of the Haida*, *The Story of the Iroquois*, and *The Story of the Navajo*, as well as beginning-to-read biographies of *Pontiac* and *Osceola*.